Original title:
Love Under the Microscope

Author: Liisi Lendorav
ISBN HARDBACK: 978-9916-89-298-5
ISBN PAPERBACK: 978-9916-89-299-2
ISBN EBOOK: 978-9916-89-300-5

The Poetry of the Particular

In the whisper of leaves, secrets unfold,
A tapestry woven, both silent and bold.
Each petal that dances in sunlight's embrace,
Holds stories of beauty, a delicate trace.

The crack of a branch, a memory shared,
Resonates softly, for those who have cared.
In shadows that linger, the past intertwines,
A narrative woven in nature's designs.

The dew on the grass, a glimmering light,
Mirrors the moments that flicker from sight.
Each heartbeat of rhythm, a pulse of the earth,
In the quiet of dawn, we remember our worth.

The glint of an eye can hold worlds untold,
In laughter and tears, a warmth to behold.
These fragments of life, both simple and clear,
Whisper the poems that dwell in our sphere.

In the poetry written in small, tender sighs,
Lies the power to lift us, to make our hearts rise.
Each detail a stanza, a note in our song,
The beauty of particular carries us along.

Two Hearts in High Resolution

In a world where pixels shine,
Two hearts merge, soft and divine.
Each glance a vivid melody,
Painting love's own symphony.

Through screens, emotions intertwine,
Captured moments, so sublime.
In high resolution's embrace,
We find our sacred space.

Every touch, a spark ignites,
Translating warmth to endless nights.
As laughter dances in the light,
Two hearts soar, taking flight.

Turns of the Tiniest Tides

Whispers of the ocean's breath,
A tide of feelings, life and death.
Each wave a turn of soft regret,
In moonlit schemes, our hearts are met.

Little ripples, secrets flow,
In quiet corners, roots will grow.
For every change, a radio plays,
Reminding us of the small ways.

The seashell sings a tuneful lore,
Of love that's danced from shore to shore.
With every turn, the heart confides,
In timeless waltzes, tiny tides.

Unveiling Affection

Unveiling shy smiles in the dusk,
In gentle moments, love's sweet musk.
Cloaked in shyness, hearts parade,
With every glance, our fears cascade.

Wrapped in silence, we reside,
Each heartbeat a tender guide.
Through layers thin, our truths appear,
With whispered hopes, we draw near.

The world fades to a muted hue,
As we unveil what is so true.
In soft embraces, we confide,
Unveiling the love we cannot hide.

The Spectrum of Affection

In colors bright, our love unfolds,
A canvas rich with stories told.
From deep indigo to radiant gold,
The spectrum of affection, bold.

Brushstrokes gentle, strokes that rhyme,
Every moment, a dance in time.
Violets blend with shades of bliss,
Signature strokes in every kiss.

The palette shifts, emotions surge,
In every heartbeat, love will merge.
A masterpiece we shape and frame,
The spectrum of affection, our eternal flame.

The Delicate Balance of Us

In tides of laughter, we drift and sway,
A dance of shadows, in light we play.
Each glance a whisper, a fragile thread,
We balance our hearts, on words unsaid.

With hopes like feathers, they float and glide,
In storms of doubt, we must confide.
A heartbeat echoes, the rhythm of trust,
We navigate love, it's a must.

Through seasons changing, we grow and bend,
In moments fleeting, where time won't end.
A fragile balance, a sacred art,
We draw the lines, to shield the heart.

When silence lingers, and shadows loom,
We find our shelter, in the same room.
In the space between us, we learn to see,
The delicate balance, of you and me.

Synapses of Shared Secrets

In fleeting glances, our stories weave,
A tapestry of whispers, we believe.
The spark of thought, ignites the night,
In synaptic dances, we find our light.

With every heartbeat, a secret shared,
An unspoken bond, that shows we cared.
Like constellations, our minds align,
In shadows of thought, our dreams entwine.

Through laughter echoing, in moments rare,
We paint our canvas, beyond compare.
In whispers soft, our truths will linger,
As hands entwined, we know the finger.

In fleeting moments, we dare to trust,
The weight of silence, a sacred must.
In nuanced gestures, our history flows,
In synapses firing, our essence shows.

The Delicate Balance of Us

In tides of laughter, we drift and sway,
A dance of shadows, in light we play.
Each glance a whisper, a fragile thread,
We balance our hearts, on words unsaid.

With hopes like feathers, they float and glide,
In storms of doubt, we must confide.
A heartbeat echoes, the rhythm of trust,
We navigate love, it's a must.

Through seasons changing, we grow and bend,
In moments fleeting, where time won't end.
A fragile balance, a sacred art,
We draw the lines, to shield the heart.

When silence lingers, and shadows loom,
We find our shelter, in the same room.
In the space between us, we learn to see,
The delicate balance, of you and me.

Synapses of Shared Secrets

In fleeting glances, our stories weave,
A tapestry of whispers, we believe.
The spark of thought, ignites the night,
In synaptic dances, we find our light.

With every heartbeat, a secret shared,
An unspoken bond, that shows we cared.
Like constellations, our minds align,
In shadows of thought, our dreams entwine.

Through laughter echoing, in moments rare,
We paint our canvas, beyond compare.
In whispers soft, our truths will linger,
As hands entwined, we know the finger.

In fleeting moments, we dare to trust,
The weight of silence, a sacred must.
In nuanced gestures, our history flows,
In synapses firing, our essence shows.

In Vitro, In Vows

In the lab of dreams, where hopes ignite,
We cultivate love, in tender light.
With trials and triumphs, our spirits grow,
In the petri dish, what will we sow?

With cells of passion, we form and fuse,
In the warmth of trust, we choose our views.
Each vow a promise, a careful plan,
In the process of love, we take a stand.

Through storms of doubt, and breezes fair,
We experiment with a love laid bare.
In the end, we'll find, what we create,
In vitro hopes, will not be late.

As swirls of laughter fill up the air,
We nurture each other, with utmost care.
In the lab of hearts, our visions grow,
With every heartbeat, the world will know.

Observations of a Heart

With gentle gazes, we watch the world,
In quiet moments, our hearts unfurled.
Each pulse a journey, a tale untold,
In observations, our love takes hold.

Through windows open, to thoughts profound,
In whispered dreams, our futures found.
We map the constellations of our soul,
In moments fleeting, we feel whole.

With every heartbeat, a lesson learned,
In shadows cast, our passions burned.
In quiet corners, where secrets lie,
We chart the paths, where feelings fly.

Through storms and sun, we stand apart,
Yet always together, never to part.
In observations made, with love as guide,
Our hearts entwined, forever abide.

Magnified Memories

In the quiet corners of my mind,
Flickering shadows intertwined.
Moments carved in timeless grace,
Embers glow in a sacred space.

Every laugh and every tear,
Resonates, always near.
A tapestry of stolen days,
Woven close in faded ways.

When the world turns cold and grey,
I find warmth in yesterday.
Echoes of a gentle sigh,
Where love and memories lie.

Candles burn with whispers sweet,
Holding all that's bittersweet.
Every glance, a cherished find,
Etched forever, heart and mind.

Through the lens of time we see,
Fragments of our history.
Each moment, a treasure trove,
In the vaults of hearts that love.

Unraveling the Threads of Us

In the loom of shared desires,
We weave dreams that never tire.
Each thread a story, bold and true,
Interlaced, me and you.

Fingers clutching, soft as air,
Whispers floating everywhere.
In the fabric of our gaze,
Love unfolds in vibrant ways.

Picking fragments from the past,
Striving for a bond that lasts.
Every challenge, every fear,
Strengthens what we hold most dear.

Patterns dance like swirling leaves,
In the tapestry we weave.
With every twist, we redefine,
The beauty of your heart in mine.

Threads unravel, yet we hold tight,
Painting shadows into light.
In the fibers of our trust,
Forever we will find our must.

Close Encounters of the Heart

Beneath the stars, where silence dwells,
Two souls dance, igniting spells.
Eyes collide in cosmic flare,
Whispers linger in the air.

With every heartbeat, time suspends,
In this moment, where love blends.
Fingers brush through midnight's veil,
A gentle story starts to sail.

In the warmth of a shared breath,
We find a bond that conquers death.
Every look speaks volumes loud,
In this place, we're free, unbowed.

Close encounters in dreamlike haze,
Lost together in a maze.
Every sigh a promise shared,
In this dance, we are declared.

In light of moons and twilight skies,
Our heartbeats echo, intertwine.
In the soft glow, our spirits soar,
Embracing love forevermore.

Quantum Particles of Passion

In the depths of fleeting grace,
Particles collide in infinite space.
Every glance, a spark ignites,
A dance of physics, wild delights.

Entangled moments, hearts on fire,
Reaching higher with each desire.
In the chaos, we both find,
The order where two hearts align.

Waves of longing, currents flow,
In this universe, love will grow.
Every heartbeat an energy wave,
Together, we are bold and brave.

As we spiral through the night,
Chaos gives way to pure light.
In the quanta where we meet,
Passion pulses, bittersweet.

With every breath, the dance of fate,
Quantum love, we celebrate.
In this realm of endless dreams,
We are more than what it seems.

The Compounds of Emotion

In whispers soft, feelings blend,
A potion brewed, where hearts ascend.
Joy and sorrow dance entwined,
In every drop, our souls confined.

A dash of laughter, a pinch of pain,
Stirred in silence, sweet as rain.
The spectrum wide, a vibrant hue,
Each moment, a story we imbue.

From love's embrace to fear's caress,
In every heartbeat, we confess.
A chemistry that knows no bounds,
In fleeting glances, truth resounds.

Through tears we grow, through joy we bind,
The compounds formed, all intertwined.
In every sigh, in every tear,
The essence of what we hold dear.

So cherish each mixture, rare and true,
For in this alchemy lies me and you.
In vials of memories, bright and dim,
The compounds of love, forever brim.

Under the Glass Slide

Beneath the lens, a world unfolds,
Tiny tales in focus, bold.
Life's intricate dance on display,
In shadows cast, the light holds sway.

Petals glisten, dew drops gleam,
Captured moments, like a dream.
Every grain, a universe wide,
Under the glass, we confide.

Cells divide, in patterns unique,
In silent stories, they speak.
A drop of water, a single thread,
In every facet, wonders spread.

Through the scope, we peer and probe,
Finding magic in the globe.
Details hidden from our sight,
Under the glass, pure delight.

A journey small, yet vast in scope,
In every sample, a whisper of hope.
So marvel at what lies in view,
Under the glass, life feels new.

Heartfelt Experiments

In the lab of dreams, we play,
Mixing wishes day by day.
A dash of kindness, a sprinkle of care,
In each experiment, love is laid bare.

We measure trust with fragile scales,
Recording laughter, where joy prevails.
Each heartbeat's rhythm, a unique sound,
In this heartfelt space, we are unbound.

Through trials and tests, we learn and grow,
In every failure, the seeds we sow.
The essence of love, a curious test,
In moments of doubt, we find our best.

With every tear, a chance to mend,
In heartfelt experiments, we transcend.
New insights gained, as we collide,
In the chemistry of hearts, love's our guide.

So mix your dreams, let passions ignite,
In this lab of ours, everything feels right.
For in each trial, a story's spun,
Heartfelt experiments are never done.

Infinite Layers of Connection

In depths unknown, we intertwine,
Infinite layers, yours and mine.
Through boundless ties, our spirits soar,
Each stream a path, forevermore.

Threads of laughter, strands of tears,
Weaving memories through the years.
In every bond, an echo found,
Infinite layers, tightly wound.

In silence shared, in words unspoken,
The fabric of trust remains unbroken.
Through trials faced, we stand as one,
In this vast web, we have begun.

With every heartbeat, currents flow,
In the depths of connection, we grow.
A tapestry rich with colors bright,
Infinite layers, pure delight.

So cherish the links that bind us tight,
In this dance of souls, we take flight.
For in each layer, love's reflection,
In infinite layers, find connection.

Exploring Affinities

In the quiet of the night,
We share our subtle dreams,
Paths entwine like vines,
In whispers, truth redeems.

With every laugh and tear,
A bond begins to grow,
Tracing lines of friendship,
In the heart's gentle flow.

Every look tells a tale,
In glances, worlds aligned,
Woven threads of purpose,
In the fabric of the mind.

Underneath the stars' glow,
Our spirits dance and sway,
Finding joy in moments,
Together, come what may.

Exploring the depths of us,
In silence, we confide,
Embracing sweet affinities,
With love as our guide.

The Essence in Details

In the shimmer of the dusk,
Lies beauty softly spread,
A petal's quiet grace,
In colors, dreams are bred.

Each brushstroke tells a story,
Of moments lost in time,
In laughter and in sorrow,
The heartbeat of a rhyme.

A dance of fleeting shadows,
In the light we seek to find,
Every detail sings a song,
In the echo of the mind.

Through the lens of our knowing,
Life reveals its sacred art,
In the essence of the simple,
We uncover every heart.

Details whisper softly,
In a world so grand and wide,
Finding meaning in the little,
Where the soul can safely bide.

Graphs of Emotion

In metrics of the heart,
We navigate the soul's map,
Tracing lines of longing,
In an ever-shifting lap.

Each smile, a data point,
Each tear, a plotted line,
In the graph of our journey,
The highs and lows entwine.

We measure love in moments,
In the scale of soft embrace,
The curves of deep connection,
Painted on life's canvas space.

Through peaks of joy and valleys,
In every rise and fall,
Graphs of emotion whisper,
In silence, we hear the call.

Together we decode,
This intricate display,
In the language of our hearts,
We find our own unique way.

A Cluster of Togetherness

In the garden of our lives,
We bloom like flowers bright,
Each petal holds a story,
In the warmth of shared light.

Entwined like roots beneath,
Our spirits intertwine,
In a cluster of togetherness,
Our hearts forever shine.

Through seasons, we will thrive,
In laughter, we find grace,
With hands held tight in joy,
In this beautiful place.

The storms may come and go,
But we stand side by side,
In unity, we're stronger,
In love, we shall abide.

A cluster forming stories,
In the fabric of each day,
Together through all journeys,
In harmony, we stay.

Infinitesimal Connections

In silence, sparks begin to weave,
Threads so thin, they barely breathe.
Across the void, a whisper flows,
A bond unseen, yet deeply grows.

Fleeting glances in crowded space,
Moments shared without a trace.
An echo forms, a pulse so light,
In tiny realms, they ignite.

Atoms dance in rhythmic sway,
Unraveled paths in night and day.
With every breath, the calm expands,
A universe held in our hands.

Microcosms intertwine sans end,
A journey where the edges blend.
In the smallest, a vast expanse,
Life reclaims its gentle dance.

Secrets held in quiet hues,
Life's resonance in tender cues.
Infinitesimal, yet profound,
In connection, all is found.

The Science of Affection

Chemistry flows in heartbeats' race,
In every breath, a warm embrace.
Molecules twine in sweet couture,
Crafting bonds both strong and pure.

Biology speaks in silent words,
Love ignites like soaring birds.
In every glance, reactions spark,
In soft touches, light fills the dark.

Neurons fire in layered thoughts,
Mapping feelings that time forgot.
With every laugh, every sigh,
The science of love will never die.

From chemistry to gentle touch,
The heart's rhythm says so much.
In sync we dance, we pulse, we pair,
A true equation, rare and fair.

In the lab of life we find,
Affection's art is intertwined.
With every beat, a story told,
In love's formula, we're consoled.

Through the Lens of Longing

In twilight's gaze, the shadows blend,
A distant call, a whispered end.
Through glassy eyes, the world reframes,
Each heartbeat calls, ignites the flames.

Every sigh, a fragile thread,
Woven paths where dreams have led.
In the stillness, hope cascades,
Through the lens, desire parades.

Moments captured, soft and sweet,
Yearning hearts, where spirits meet.
In quiet corners, dreams unfold,
A canvas painted, a tale retold.

Fleeting visions through the night,
In every pulse, a spark of light.
Through longing's grasp, we seek to fill,
The spaces where the heart lies still.

Portraits drawn of what could be,
Through the lens, we try to see.
In the distance, a longing song,
A symphony where we belong.

Cells of Passion

In the heart's core, passion thrives,
Cells pulsate, where love derives.
A mighty force in tender frames,
Igniting hearts, lighting flames.

Veins entwined with fiery hue,
Every heartbeat feels so true.
Cellular rhythms, sweet and strong,
Each pulse whispers a sacred song.

Within the skin, a journey flows,
Through veins, the fire's fervor grows.
Innocent glances turned to heat,
Cells of passion, where lovers meet.

In the dance of touch and breath,
Resonating, defying death.
Each kiss a spark, a bright ascent,
In every moment, time is spent.

Love's chemistry, a grand display,
In each cell, it finds its way.
Passion flows in vibrant streams,
In every heartbeat, woven dreams.

Captured Chemistry in Detail

In the lab, reactions spark,
Atoms dance, igniting the dark.
Mixing elements, a blend so fine,
In every drop, we see the design.

Beakers bubble, secrets unfold,
Molecules whisper, stories told.
An alchemist's dream, a painter's brush,
Creating wonders, in that quiet hush.

With each experiment, a new delight,
Capturing moments, pure and bright.
Science unfolds like petals of spring,
In the heart of matter, life takes wing.

The bonds we form, the ties we weave,
In chemical chaos, we believe.
A symphony played in beakers and flasks,
To unveil the beauty of nature's tasks.

In their embrace, we find the truth,
Nature's wisdom, the joys of youth.
Captured in detail, a precious sight,
In every reaction, there shines a light.

Radiating Warmth—Cell by Cell

In bodies vast, warmth does flow,
Cells connect, as spirits grow.
Tiny sparks in muted night,
Together they share their light.

Signals sent, electric beats,
In rhythm, the heart repeats.
Through veins and tissues, whispers glide,
Nature's warmth, our faithful guide.

Mitochondria, power within,
Fueling life as moments spin.
Each heartbeat echoes, soft and clear,
In unity's dance, we persevere.

From cell to cell, a bond so pure,
In shared existence, we endure.
Waves of comfort, in silence bloom,
Radiating warmth, dispelling gloom.

In every touch, in every breath,
Life weaves the tapestry of death.
Cell by cell, a journey vast,
In every present lies the past.

Infinitesimal Connections

In the smallest bits, a world unfolds,
Connections linger, stories told.
Atoms entangled in a cosmic thread,
In the unseen, our hearts are led.

Through silence speaks the universe' voice,
In tiniest details, we find our choice.
Subtle gestures, a knowing glance,
In infinitesimals, we take our chance.

Moments colliding, a spark ignites,
In the unseen dance, we find our sights.
Particles whisper, a language of old,
Binding us all, both timid and bold.

In the fabric of life, delicate weave,
Invisible bonds, we dare to believe.
Every heartbeat, every sigh,
Infinitesimal blessings, as time slips by.

With every breath, we intertwine,
In the smallest realms, design divine.
Connections made, while shadows play,
In every heartbeat, a grand ballet.

Fractal Patterns of Togetherness

In nature's maze, patterns arise,
Infinite beauty, beneath the skies.
Fractals dance, in symmetry spread,
Each detail reveals what lies ahead.

Like branches weave, so lives entwine,
In every echo, a chance to shine.
A spiral of life, endlessly turns,
In soft whispers, the spirit yearns.

Each moment shapes the path we trace,
In shapes and colors, we find our place.
Together we grow, a vibrant thread,
In tangled roots, dreams are fed.

From mountains high to valleys low,
In unity's grasp, together we grow.
Fractal patterns, a cosmic play,
In every heartbeat, life's grand display.

Interconnected, we rise and fall,
In the tapestry of life, we have it all.
Fractal patterns, ever-shifting form,
In the unity of being, we are born.

Spectrum of Shared Moments

In soft hues of laughter, we find our way,
Moments in silence, where words never stray.
Every glance whispers what hearts want to say,
Captured in time, in the light of the day.

Colors blend deeply, in shades we create,
Stories unfold, as we navigate fate.
Together we wander, no need to debate,
In the spectrum of trust, we both resonate.

Golden warmth glimmers, in each fleeting glance,
Cascading memories, an eternal dance.
Hand in hand, moving, entranced by the chance,
We build a canvas, our love is the stance.

Underneath starlight, our spirits align,
Charting the constellations, hearts intertwine.
With every heartbeat, like echoes, we shine,
In the spectrum of shared moments, divine.

Exploring Affection's Blueprint

Amid the chaos, we sketch our desires,
Blueprints of love, igniting the fires.
With each gentle touch, the heart slowly tires,
Drafting the plans, where affection inspires.

Lines intertwine in a delicate trace,
Mapping the contours of each warm embrace.
With colors of passion, we fill up the space,
In exploring affection, we find our grace.

Dimensions of closeness expand and evolve,
Solving the puzzles that life does resolve.
In blueprints of truth, our hearts do involve,
Together constructing the world we dissolve.

Yet storms may arise, and shadows may sway,
But our solid structure will always stay.
With love as our compass, we know the way,
Exploring affection, come what may.

Chemical Reactions of the Heart

In the lab of emotions, we mix and we blend,
Reactions unknown, where feelings extend.
With every small glance, the energies spend,
Chemical treasures that never will end.

Bubbles of laughter, a volatile mix,
Bonding like atoms, our hearts begin tricks.
Catalysts dance, and the tension then shifts,
Awakening senses, pure joy as it clicks.

Formulae written in whispers and sighs,
Responding to chemistry found in our eyes.
No science can measure the love that defies,
In the reactions of hearts, the truth never lies.

We spark with each touch, igniting anew,
Creating compounds and bonds just for two.
In this laboratory, where love is our view,
The chemical reactions, forever true.

Petals of Emotion

In gardens of feelings, we walk hand in hand,
Petals of emotion, a vibrant expanse.
Each bloom tells a story, like grains of sand,
Scattering memories in love's gentle dance.

Whispers of springtime, fresh fragrance in air,
Delicate moments, sweet traces we share.
With colors united, in love's moistened care,
Petals of emotion, a tapestry rare.

Through seasons of change, as petals may fall,
New buds will awaken, and beauty enthrall.
In cycles of life, we embrace every call,
Petals of emotion, we cherish them all.

So let us keep nurturing this blossoming art,
In the garden of love, where we each take part.
With roots intertwined, never drifting apart,
Petals of emotion blossom from the heart.

Dissecting Devotion

In the quiet hours of night,
I ponder all our shared delight.
Each word spoken, a gentle sway,
In whispered dreams, we find our way.

The core of love lies deep within,
A tender place where we begin.
With every glance, the world aligns,
A tapestry of souls that shine.

Moments caught in fragile glass,
Time stands still, as shadows pass.
Every heartbeat, a silent call,
Together we rise, together we fall.

Love's anatomy laid bare, so true,
Each layer crafted, only for you.
In every scar, a story told,
In our embrace, a warmth unfolds.

Dissecting fragments, piece by piece,
In our connection, we find release.
Devotion blooms in subtle art,
An endless rhythm, soul to heart.

Heartstrings under Analysis

Tangled threads, a symphony,
Playing softly, both you and me.
Notes of laughter, tears and sighs,
A melody that never dies.

Mapping out the ties we weave,
In every moment, we believe.
Chords that resonate, softly hum,
In this dance, we've just begun.

Pulling on those heartstrings tight,
Guided by the stars at night.
Every twist reveals a truth,
In the chords of timeless youth.

Dismissed doubts fade away,
When together, we choose to stay.
In the rhythm of our embrace,
We find comfort, our sacred space.

Heartstrings sing, a gentle tune,
Binding us beneath the moon.
Evolving love, a canvas bright,
Painted in layers of pure light.

Neurons of Affection

Electrical impulses, swift and bright,
Firing fast, igniting the night.
Every glance a spark of flame,
In the dance, we find our name.

Waves of warmth flow through the air,
Connection blooms, beyond compare.
In every touch, a signal sent,
Neurons firing, the heart's intent.

Intense currents, deep and true,
Mapping pathways from me to you.
Synapses crackle with pure delight,
In this maze, our souls take flight.

Complex circuits intertwine,
In this chaos, we draw the line.
Love, a language we both know,
In still waters, emotions flow.

Neurons whirl, a cosmic thread,
In the silence, whispers spread.
Affection's pulse beats strong and clear,
Binding us close, forever near.

The Pulse of Togetherness

In the heartbeat of shared space,
Resonating, a sacred grace.
With every thrum, a bond so tight,
In sync we move, a dance of light.

Time slows down in moments small,
Each pulse echoing love's sweet call.
Together we journey, hand in hand,
Writing stories in the sand.

The rhythm of laughter fills the air,
In the quiet, we find our care.
Pulse of life, steady and strong,
In this melody, we both belong.

With each breath, a new embrace,
Echoing love in every trace.
In togetherness, we've found our song,
A harmony where hearts belong.

The pulse beats on, a lasting fire,
Fuelled by dreams, and pure desire.
Together we thrive, an endless quest,
In the heartbeat of love, we are blessed.

Romantic Reactions

In the silence of the night,
Two hearts beat in rhythm tight.
Whispers soft, like a gentle breeze,
Entangled souls, forever at ease.

Eyes meet, igniting a spark,
A journey begins, with love as the mark.
Laughter blooms, painting the air,
With every glance, we lay our hearts bare.

Hands entwined, like vines that climb,
Creating a story, transcending time.
In every touch, a universe flows,
In this dance, true passion grows.

Moments shared, as time slips away,
In your gaze, the stars brightly play.
All the chaos, fades to a calm,
In the embrace, I find my balm.

With every heartbeat, with every sigh,
Love's sweet chemistry, we will not deny.
Through life's kaleidoscope, we will soar,
Together forever, to explore more.

In the Smallest Spaces

In a crowded room, our eyes collide,
A universe blooms, where secrets reside.
The smallest smile, a spark ignites,
In shared silence, the world ignites.

A brush of hands, electric and bold,
Whispers hidden, waiting to be told.
In the nooks where shadows play,
Love finds a way, come what may.

Between the words, magic lingers,
Lost in thoughts, the heart's soft singers.
Tiny moments, blossoming bright,
Creating galaxies, with pure delight.

In the quiet, our spirits dance,
In the smallest spaces, we find our chance.
With every glance, the world recedes,
In love's embrace, the heart proceeds.

In a gentle touch, we define our fate,
In the smallest spaces, love opens the gate.
Together we journey, wherever it leads,
Two souls intertwined, fulfilling their needs.

The Quark of Romance

In the nucleus of our hearts,
Love's energy quietly starts.
A quark of joy, spinning around,
In the core of us, warmth is found.

Like particles in a cosmic dance,
In gravity's pull, we take a chance.
In every moment, forces collide,
Creating a bond, love cannot hide.

The universe whispers the sweetest tune,
Underneath the silver moon.
In the realm of dreams, we drift and sway,
Chasing the dusk, embracing the day.

Quarks of laughter, charges align,
In your embrace, I feel divine.
With every heartbeat, atoms connect,
In the fabric of love, we reflect.

Through space and time, we journey far,
In a celestial dance, we become a star.
The quark of romance, forever will stay,
Binding us close, come what may.

Chemistry of Connection

In the laboratory of our hearts,
Chemistry blooms, where love imparts.
Molecules dance in perfect sync,
Creating a bond, stronger than we think.

In the test tubes of time, we brew,
Experiments of trust, just me and you.
With every laugh, reactions ignite,
Fueling our fire, burning bright.

Hydrogen and oxygen blend,
In a formula, where hearts transcend.
In the flasks of hope, we find our way,
With each connection, love's grand display.

Electrons swirl in joyous flight,
Through the elements, we find our light.
With careful measure, we craft our fate,
In love's lab, we celebrate.

In the chemistry of connection, we reside,
In every heartbeat, love's truth we confide.
Together we create, a masterpiece rare,
In the bond we share, we find our prayer.

Microscopic Moments

In the world unseen, we tread,
Wonders bloom, quiet and spread.
A drop of water, life does hold,
Stories whispers, waiting to unfold.

Beneath the lens, a dance begins,
Life's subtleties, where magic spins.
Cells entwined in a gentle waltz,
Nature's art, devoid of faults.

Tiny figures, shadows play,
In the twilight, vibrant array.
A single breath, the stillness breaks,
In the silence, the heart awakes.

Whispers of existence, pure and grand,
Moments captured, as if planned.
Glances exchanged, worlds collide,
In each heartbeat, life won't hide.

Every detail, a tale it seems,
In microscopic dreams we gleam.
Life's essence, we strive to see,
In the minute, we find the key.

Grand Feelings

Mountains rise above the sea,
Painted skies hold dreams so free.
Whispers echo through the pine,
In every moment, hearts align.

The rush of waves, a gentle song,
In nature's cradle, we belong.
Stars above, like eyes that gleam,
In the dark, we chase a dream.

Hands entwined on paths we roam,
With every step, we build our home.
Softest breezes, tender sighs,
In the silence, love never dies.

Time can fold like pages worn,
In grand feelings, we are reborn.
Each heartbeat, a thunderous call,
In love's embrace, we stand tall.

While life sways in quiet grace,
We find our strength in this vast space.
In laughter shared, and tears defined,
The grandest feelings, forever entwined.

The Fine Line Between You and Me.

A thread so thin, a whispered breath,
Between our souls, life and death.
Moments linger like summer's haze,
In each glance, a heartfelt phase.

Bound by shadows, light does tease,
In silence shared, we find our ease.
Fingers brushing, electric air,
The fine line blurs, a mutual dare.

Words unspoken dance in the night,
Guiding us toward a new light.
In every step, boundaries bend,
On this journey, hearts transcend.

Trust is fragile, like morning dew,
In every word, the truth feels new.
With every sigh, time draws us near,
In the delicate balance, love appears.

So take my hand, let's walk this line,
Between the stars, our hearts align.
For in this moment, so sweet and free,
Exists the beauty of you and me.

A Closer Examination of the Heart

In the depths of tender beats,
Hidden chambers where love greets.
Each thump a story, yearning sighs,
With every pulse, truth implies.

Delicate whispers in shadows play,
Mapping out feelings along the way.
Veins of hope, flowing sincere,
In every tear, love's shadow near.

Open closely, let layers peel,
In layers deep, emotions feel.
With gentle hands, we extract the core,
Finding the essence, always wanting more.

The map of longing, etched in time,
Sings a ballad, soft and sublime.
In the silence, the heart's design,
A closer look makes love align.

So linger here, in this gentle art,
Together we'll face a brand new start.
In every heartbeat, we shall find,
A treasure deep, soul intertwined.

Tiny Flames in a Petri Dish

In glass confines, they flicker bright,
Tiny flames, a dance of light.
Life ignites in a small expanse,
In this world, they take a chance.

Growth unfolds, fragile and bold,
Unseen magic in stories told.
Cells collide with vibrant zest,
In this dish, they find their quest.

A spark of life, in shadows cast,
Moments held, forever last.
Careful eyes watch every turn,
In this warmth, young passions burn.

Brave endeavors, tiny and sweet,
Life's beginnings in heartfelt beat.
Whispers of hope, a chance to thrive,
In every flicker, dreams come alive.

So nurture these flames, let them soar,
In the chaos, find what's more.
For in this petri dish, we see,
The beauty of life's fragility.

Microcosm of Desire

In shadows cast by candlelight,
Whispers dance, unseen yet bright.
Hearts aflame, the echoes call,
In the silence, we unfold it all.

Dreams collide like stars at night,
Paths entwined, love takes flight.
A universe within each gaze,
In every longing, a secret phrase.

Fingers brush, a spark ignites,
Moments pause, the world ignites.
In the stillness, passion swells,
A tale of two, in silence tells.

Desire's thread, a golden seam,
Woven deep in every dream.
A microcosm, vast and true,
Each heartbeat belongs to you.

In tender glances, worlds are spun,
Each breath taken, we become one.
A symphony of heartbeats plays,
In this dance, forever stays.

Beneath the Surface of Us

Beneath the waves, where secrets lie,
A hidden depth, a whispered sigh.
The currents pull, entwined we flow,
In waters deep, our true selves show.

Rippling thoughts beneath the skin,
A maze of dreams where we begin.
Surface calm, yet storms can rise,
In silent depths, our truth belies.

Each heartbeat carries tales unspoken,
In gentle cradles, bonds unbroken.
With every glance, we dive anew,
A world unseen, just me and you.

Reefs of hope in shadowed light,
Together we ignite the night.
In depths of trust, we learn to swim,
Beneath the surface, love won't dim.

The tide may pull, but we remain,
In this embrace, we bear the strain.
Beneath the waves, our spirits soar,
Together always, forevermore.

Two Souls through the Glass

Through glass we gaze, reflections clear,
Two souls adrift, yet ever near.
In every glance, a world ignites,
As shadows blend in soft moonlight.

The distance feels both vast and small,
In fragile frames, we find it all.
A silent promise, a knowing smile,
In mirrored realms, we bridge the mile.

A touch of hands, though miles apart,
Each heartbeat echoes, a work of art.
Through crystal panes, our spirits dance,
In the space between, we take our chance.

Every tear, a story shared,
In the silence, the heart laid bared.
Two souls entwined in a fleeting glance,
Through glass we find our sweet romance.

In dreams we walk, side by side,
In whispered hopes, we learn to abide.
Two souls through glass, forever free,
In every shimmer, it's you and me.

The Science of Sentiment

In tiny atoms of emotions spun,
A chemistry of hearts begun.
Neurons fire, connections made,
In every glance, the fears allayed.

The heart, a vessel, beats in time,
With rhythms soft, a tender rhyme.
In laughter shared and tears that flow,
The science crafted, love will grow.

We analyze the pulse of fate,
Each heartbeat sings, we celebrate.
In formulas of joy and pain,
Through every loss, we love again.

The bond we share, a mystery vast,
In every moment, shadows cast.
Through trials faced and battles won,
In the lab of life, our love's begun.

So let us measure, let us learn,
In every lesson, hearts will yearn.
The science of sentiment entwined,
In every pulse, our love defined.

Minuscule Moments

A fleeting glance shared in the light,
Soft whispers drift, tender and bright.
Small joys collected like morning dew,
Each heartbeat whispers, 'I see you.'

A child's laugh rings, sweet and clear,
Time stands still when you're near.
Days may tumble like leaves in fall,
Yet these moments, we cherish them all.

A gentle touch, a knowing smile,
Weaving memories, mile by mile.
In seconds wrapped, life starts to gleam,
Minuscule moments, a shared dream.

Sunset paints the sky in hues,
Simple pleasures, the heart's muse.
Beneath the stars, where wishes dwell,
Life's sweet secrets, we know them well.

So hold on tight to these tiny things,
Like fragile feathers on hopeful wings.
In every breath, in every sigh,
Minuscule moments never say goodbye.

Refined Affection

In the quiet dawn, our fingers meet,
A gentle warmth, our hearts in beat.
Through laughter and tears, we find our way,
Refined affection grows day by day.

Shared glances that linger, whispers so sweet,
A dance of souls, where love feels complete.
In the chaos, a soothing grace,
Each moment shared, a warm embrace.

A soft caress, a brush of skin,
In every heartbeat, where love begins.
The world may rush, yet we stand still,
Refined affection, a sacred thrill.

When storms may rage and shadows fall,
We find our refuge, we hear love's call.
In silent depths, where true hearts dwell,
Refined affection, a tale to tell.

So let us nurture, let love grow,
In the softness of night, let our hearts glow.
With every touch, let our spirits soar,
Refined affection, forevermore.

The Behavior of Bonding

In crowded rooms, a spark ignites,
Connection blooms, soft and bright.
Words like threads weave hearts together,
The behavior of bonding, light as a feather.

Each shared secret, a promise made,
In laughter's echo, fears will fade.
The dance of souls, an intricate art,
Where moments thrive and never part.

Through trials faced and dreams pursued,
In this vast world, we're never subdued.
With every challenge, unity grows,
The behavior of bonding, like rivers flows.

In silence shared, our souls confide,
With hands entwined, there's no divide.
A tapestry rich, woven with care,
The behavior of bonding, forever rare.

So let us treasure, this gift we bear,
In every smile, in every prayer.
For love unites, in a vibrant song,
The behavior of bonding, where we belong.

Impulses and Atoms

In the quiet hum of the night,
Impulses spark, igniting light.
Tiny atoms dance, collide,
In the rhythm of life, they cannot hide.

Moments flash, a heartbeat's thrill,
Emotions pulse, with every quill.
In the chaos of thought, we find our way,
Impulses and atoms, in a grand ballet.

Each fleeting thought, a flicker bright,
Connections form in the still of night.
In whispers soft, we feel the beat,
Impulses weave a tapestry sweet.

With every breath, a world is spun,
Atoms collide, creation begun.
In every glance, in every sigh,
Impulses and atoms, together they fly.

So embrace the rush, let feelings roam,
In the heart of chaos, we find our home.
With every pulse, love's anthem sings,
Impulses and atoms, the joy it brings.

Emotions in Focus

In the quiet corners of my heart,
Tender whispers dance, a silent art.
Joy and sorrow blend like daylight,
Emotions swirling, taking flight.

Moments stolen, fleeting, rare,
Joyful laughter fills the air.
In shadows deep, the pain resides,
Yet hope still glimmers, love abides.

Like colors splashed upon a page,
Each feeling a story, a silent stage.
From the depths, I rise and fall,
Emotions echoing, a haunting call.

Glimmers of passion, shadows of doubt,
In this canvas, I am laid out.
Each heartbeat a signal, a soft refrain,
Emotions vivid, alive with pain.

In the twilight of dreams unfurled,
I capture the essence of my world.
Through laughter and tears, I find my way,
In emotions' grip, I choose to stay.

Close Encounters of the Tender Kind

In soft glances, our eyes entwine,
Gentle touches, the world feels fine.
Hearts collide in a silent dance,
Close encounters spark a chance.

Whispers linger, sweet and low,
In the warmth, our feelings grow.
Moments cherished, time stands still,
Tender secrets shared at will.

Underneath the starlit sky,
Promises made with a heartfelt sigh.
Hands entwined, we wander free,
In each heartbeat, you and me.

Every shared laugh, a thread we weave,
In this tapestry, we believe.
With every pause, our souls align,
Tender moments, your heart in mine.

As the dawn breaks, colors blend,
In every heartbeat, love transcends.
Through close encounters, we ignite,
A tender bond, pure and bright.

Reflections in a Drop of Tears

In a solitary tear, a story lies,
Reflections murmur, silent cries.
Each droplet holds a world immense,
Echoes of joy, pain intense.

Shimmering gently, it embraces light,
A canvas of memories, day and night.
In the stillness, truths reveal,
The depth of sorrow, the weight we feel.

Lost in thought, I trace the path,
Amidst the pain, I find the laugh.
Through the lens of sorrow's grace,
I glimpse the love, the warm embrace.

Each tear a mirror, a glimpse within,
Carrying the weight, the loss, the win.
Reflections dance in the gentle glow,
In a drop of tears, we learn to grow.

Through the storm, our hearts learn to bend,
In every tear, beginnings blend.
A cycle of healing, a soft refrain,
In reflections vast, we rise again.

Chemistry of the Soul

In the silence, sparks ignite,
Two souls paired in a cosmic light.
Chemistry blooms in every glance,
A dance of fate, a timeless chance.

Molecules of laughter fill the space,
Binding hearts in a warm embrace.
Every heartbeat a symphony,
In this potion, you and me.

With every spark, the universe spins,
A bond crafted where love begins.
In whispered secrets, two become one,
Chemistry flows, a journey begun.

Entwined in moments, pure and bright,
Together forging our shared light.
In the alchemy of trust, we find,
The chemistry of heart and mind.

Through trials faced, we shall endure,
In this fusion, we feel so sure.
In the lab of love, we freely soar,
Chemistry of the soul, forevermore.

Whispers Beneath the Lens

In shadows cast by fleeting light,
Soft secrets stir, a quiet flight.
Each glance reveals a hidden tale,
Where hearts converge, and dreams set sail.

Silk threads of time in silence weave,
In whispered hues, we learn to believe.
Through lenses clear, the world transforms,
In moments found, our love conforms.

The grainy edges blur the lines,
Where laughter dances, and hope entwines.
With every click, a story blooms,
In photographs, our essence looms.

Captured warmth in autumn's breath,
A fragile dance, defying death.
Through frames of memory, we gaze,
In each other's eyes, a timeless haze.

As light spills down and shadows play,
We carve our names in bright array.
For in each moment, brightly spent,
We frame our love, a lasting event.

Intimacy in Focus

Two souls aligned in quiet grace,
In every touch, a warm embrace.
The world fades out, we disappear,
In whispered truths, our hearts draw near.

Unraveled secrets gently shared,
In intimacy, no need to be scared.
The lens of trust reveals our core,
Our spirits dance, forevermore.

With every sigh, connection grows,
In tender spaces, true love flows.
A gentle gaze, a knowing smile,
Together we walk, mile by mile.

In fleeting glances, warmth ignites,
Our silent vows, the stars ignite.
In harmony, our rhythm beats,
An endless song where passion greets.

As shadows stretch and daylight dies,
In twilight's arms, our dream complies.
Intimacy blooms, forever sown,
In heart's embrace, we find our home.

The Anatomy of Affection

Underneath the skin, it lies,
A tender pulse that never dies.
Mapped in curves, the heart takes flight,
In every beat, a spark ignites.

Fingers trace the contours deep,
In whispered secrets that we keep.
Through layers soft, our essence glows,
In every sigh, the passion flows.

A cartographer of souls we are,
Drawing paths like ancient stars.
With every look, a universe,
In body language, love's sweet verse.

Muscles tense and hearts collide,
In this intimacy, we confide.
The anatomy of love unfolds,
In fragile moments, truth beholds.

From gentle brushes to searing fire,
Together, we dance, a fierce desire.
In every touch, a alchemy,
The essence of us, wild and free.

Petri Dish of Passion

In a world confined, we start to grow,
Amidst the shadows, the warmth will show.
Cultivated dreams in a glassy space,
In every drop, our love's embrace.

Microcosm filled with vibrant hues,
Where wild ambitions hum with clues.
Each ripple echoes, the heart ignites,
In this petri dish, our passion bites.

Stirring cultures of hope and fear,
In the quiet lab, we're always near.
The essence thick, both sweet and sour,
In every moment, we reclaim power.

Under the microscope, we collide,
In experiments where dreams reside.
Reactions sparking, a fervent dance,
In this chemistry, we take a chance.

In tiny realms, our love expands,
Creating boundaries that nature understands.
For in this dish, we find our way,
And build a love that's here to stay.

Delicate Dynamics

In the stillness of the air,
Tiny particles dance with flair.
Their movements soft, a gentle sway,
Nature's rhythm on display.

At times they clash, a brief collide,
Creating chaos, then a slide.
In every touch, a spark ignites,
The beauty found in their flights.

Glimmers of light in shadow's play,
Each whisper leaves a path to lay.
A harmony that weaves and bends,
Where every start leads to the ends.

With every pulse, a story spins,
Through quiet moments, life begins.
So delicate, the ties we feel,
In every breath, the world is real.

To dance within this hidden sphere,
Where science meets our silent fear.
The dynamics shifting slow,
In whispers, they teach us to grow.

Intertwined at the Smallest Scale

In the depths of unseen strands,
Life entangles, holds our hands.
Cells and bonds, both strong and frail,
Woven stories, silent tale.

Molecules share an ancient bond,
A dance of trust, an endless fond.
In every twist, each thread embraced,
A tapestry of time interlaced.

Among the atoms, secrets sigh,
Universes where dreams comply.
The smallest scale reveals it all,
In whispers soft, both rise and fall.

Connected tightly, hearts align,
From distant starlight, our paths combine.
A symphony of life bestowed,
In unity, our essence flowed.

Interwoven in the grand design,
In every heart, a truth divine.
The smallest scale holds vast expanse,
A world alive within this dance.

Whispers from Within

In quiet corners of the mind,
A gentle voice, elusive, kind.
Echoes of dreams softly unfurl,
Whispers that glide through our world.

Each thought like fire, flickers low,
Words that shimmer, then let go.
Stories linger, tucked away,
In shadows where the secrets sway.

Delicately weaving through the night,
Beneath the stars, they take their flight.
A symphony played on silent strings,
The heart learns what the soul brings.

When solitude holds its patient hand,
Whispers emerge like grains of sand.
They guide us to our truest form,
A refuge safe, a heart so warm.

From within, the truth will rise,
Mirrored in our own soft sighs.
In every moment, small and grand,
Whispers embrace us, understand.

Nearness in a Lab Coat

In sterile light, the world feels thin,
Each experiment, a chance to begin.
With careful hands and focused eyes,
Curiosity sparks, and science flies.

Data like whispers in the air,
Finding answers with tender care.
Graphs and charts, a dance of thought,
In lab coats, new worlds are sought.

Each test a step, a story told,
In beakers bubbling, mysteries unfold.
The clock ticks gently, patience grows,
In the chaos, a calmness flows.

Nearness felt in every task,
In shared glances, we learn to ask.
Together we seek, through trial and error,
In each small triumph, our hearts grow clearer.

Through lenses strong, we find the light,
In every struggle, beauty in sight.
In a lab coat, we bridge the divide,
Nearness unites, where dreams abide.

Fragments of Euphoria

Whispers of laughter, soft and bright,
Like stars that dance in the velvet night.
Moments gather, fleeting, bold,
In the warm embrace of dreams untold.

Echoes of joy, like shimmering streams,
Flow through the fabric of tender dreams.
Each second a jewel, a spark of grace,
In the mosaic of time, we lose our pace.

A gentle sigh on a summer breeze,
Nature's chorus, putting hearts at ease.
In every fragment, a story unfolds,
A treasure of life, more precious than gold.

In twilight's glow, hope takes its flight,
Chasing the shadows, welcoming the light.
With every heartbeat, we rise and soar,
In fragments of euphoria, we find our core.

So let us gather these pieces near,
In laughter and love, we conquer fear.
For in this dance, we ignite the flame,
Euphoria's whisper, always the same.

The Anatomy of Desire

In the quiet corners of yearning's heart,
Desire simmers, a delicate art.
It carves its path through every thought,
In shadows and echoes, love is sought.

Crimson ribbons tie dreams in knots,
Sensations linger in sacred spots.
Each glance a promise, a spark so bright,
A dance of souls in the muted light.

Measured breaths in intoxicating air,
An urge to touch, a silent dare.
With every whisper, the tension grows,
In the anatomy of desire, the heart knows.

Silent confessions under the stars,
Unveiling secrets, healing the scars.
In the tapestry of longing we weave,
Moments of truth, it's hard to believe.

Yet through this longing, we find ourselves,
In every book, on all the shelves.
For desire is more than a fleeting glance,
It's the beating drum in love's own dance.

Small Wonders of the Heart

A child's laughter, a fleeting sound,
In the simplest moments, joy is found.
A butterfly landing, soft and light,
Whispers of happiness, taking flight.

Petals falling in the gentle breeze,
Nature's beauty, small acts that please.
The sun dips low, painting skies aglow,
Each sunset a canvas, starting to show.

Hands entwined in a silent embrace,
A spark of connection, a sacred space.
These little wonders, quiet and true,
Fill the heart with colors anew.

Raindrops dancing on a window pane,
Symphonies echoing a sweet refrain.
In the softness of night, dreams ignite,
Small wonders linger, hearts take flight.

So let us cherish these moments rare,
In the small wonders, love fills the air.
For in each heartbeat, a story departs,
Celebrating the small wonders of hearts.

Heartstrings and Helices

In the labyrinth of tangled grace,
Heartstrings pull in a fervent race.
Twisting paths of love entwine,
In the dance of fate, our lives align.

Helices spiral, endlessly twined,
A fusion of souls, intricately designed.
In every touch, a spark transcends,
Binding two hearts, where the journey bends.

Through trials faced, our spirits grow,
In the garden of trust, seeds we sow.
With laughter and tears, we navigate,
The music of love, never too late.

With every heartbeat, we weave a song,
In the fabric of days, where we belong.
Heartstrings resonate, a symphony plays,
In the dance of love, we lose and amaze.

So here we stand, on life's fine line,
Heartstrings and helices, a design divine.
Forever united, through all the strife,
In the melody of love, we find our life.

Anatomy of a Heartbeat

In the quiet thrum of night,
A pulse whispers to the dark.
Rhythms weave through fragile light,
Memories dance, a waking spark.

Each beat echoes untold tales,
Stories draped in tender skin.
Life unfurls where love prevails,
Hope resides where dreams begin.

With every flutter, courage stands,
A testament both fierce and kind.
In the chambers, strength expands,
Uniting body, soul, and mind.

Wrapped in warmth, embrace the flow,
Let the heartbeat guide the way.
This is where the lovers grow,
In the rhythm of their stay.

Nature's song, both sweet and clear,
Every note, a cherished part.
Connected deeply, year by year,
The body sings, the beating heart.

Close-Up on Connection

Underneath the shadows cast,
Fingers brush, a gentle spark.
Eyes meet eyes, a moment vast,
Bridges formed within the dark.

The world outside fades away,
In this space, time seems to freeze.
Words unspoken, yet they play,
Like a whisper on the breeze.

Connection pulses, raw and true,
Electric veins, a soft embrace.
Shared laughter, tears, a vibrant hue,
Moments etched in tender grace.

In the quiet, hearts collide,
Fusion of two separate souls.
Inside this bond, we can confide,
In unity, we feel whole.

A tapestry of lives entwined,
Woven threads reveal the art.
In the intricate, we find,
The vastness of the human heart.

Fragments of a Tender Heart

Scattered pieces on the floor,
Shards of love that once were whole.
Each fragment whispers tales of yore,
Of laughter, pain, and longing stole.

In the ripples of the past,
Colors blend where echoes dwell.
Mending wounds, a love steadfast,
Healing stories yet to tell.

Homes built on a fragile stone,
Porcelain dreams that might decay.
Yet in the cracks, beauty shone,
A radiant dance of light and gray.

Through the chaos, hearts arise,
Resilient in the face of strife.
Each fragment like a shooting star,
Guides us through the maze of life.

In every heart, a tale resides,
A mosaic of joy and scars.
Together, we embrace the tides,
Finding brilliance in the stars.

Secrets in the Petri Dish

In a world where cultures blend,
Microbes dance beneath the glass.
Life emerges without an end,
Whispers of the fates that pass.

Colors bloom in hidden ways,
A secret garden, small yet wide.
In this realm, the tiny plays,
Reveal the life that dare not hide.

Each sample holds a quiet truth,
Nature's dance in every drop.
In the heart of science, youth,
Finds its voice amid the hop.

Beneath the lens, connections spark,
Patterns formed in silence sweet.
Tiny worlds, both light and dark,
Present challenges, bold and neat.

In the dish, we learn to see,
The fragile weave of life so grand.
Every secret moves to be,
A testament to Nature's hand.

A Love So Small

In shadows cast by morning light,
Two hearts whispered through the night.
Softest touches, fleeting grace,
In tiny moments, love we trace.

A glance exchanged, a shy retreat,
In the silence, pulses beat.
The smallest gestures, sweet and rare,
A world of meaning lies laid bare.

With every laugh, a spark ignites,
In simple joys, our hearts take flight.
Though words may falter, feelings grow,
A tender bond, a gentle flow.

Beneath the stars, we softly dream,
In quiet nights, love's gentle theme.
The universe in our embrace,
A love so small, yet fills the space.

So let us dance in twilight's hue,
Where love is pure, and hearts stay true.
In every heartbeat, we discover,
The beauty found in one another.

Hypotheses of the Heart

What if love's a fleeting spark,
A fleeting flame within the dark?
Theories stacked and thoughts entwined,
In every pulse, new truths we find.

Could it be fate or mere chance?
In every look, we weave romance.
The heart, a puzzle forged in time,
With every ache, a silent rhyme.

Do we create our own designs?
In whispered hopes, our dream aligns.
With every question, answers bloom,
In tender space, we find our room.

What fuels the fire of desire?
Each breath we take, a shared choir.
The syntax of love, profound,
In every laugh, our truths abound.

Is love a riddle, or a sign?
In hidden glances, stars align.
The heart unveils its mysteries,
In every beat, potential histories.

Synapses of Sentiment

From thought to thought, we make the leap,
In every silence, feelings seep.
Neurons fire with electric grace,
Connections form in time and space.

Emotions dance like flickering light,
In shadows deep, they take their flight.
Whispers of love in currents flow,
A tapestry of what we know.

With every smile, a signal sent,
A surge of joy, a sweet lament.
The mind and heart in sync collide,
In memories cherished, love won't hide.

The chemistry of us entwined,
In every heartbeat, hope defined.
Each glance ignites a vivid spark,
In this vast universe, we embark.

Through synapses, we find our way,
In paths of light, we choose to stay.
A journey shared, both near and far,
In every moment, love's our star.

Emotive Encounters

In crowded rooms, we lock our gaze,
A moment lost in life's great maze.
Emotions swirl, a vivid hue,
In heartbeat's pulse, I find you true.

When laughter sings, and sorrows fade,
We chase the light, no plans are laid.
Every step, a story made,
In every touch, our fears cascade.

With every sigh, a tale unfolds,
Of whispered dreams and secrets told.
The brush of hands, a spark ignites,
Through fleeting hours, our souls take flight.

In parting dawn, a bittersweet,
We walk away, yet love's repeat.
For in our hearts, the truth remains,
In every loss, our joy sustains.

So let us cherish, love transcends,
Through every journey, where it bends.
Emotive encounters, bright and rare,
In every moment, we're laid bare.

Heartbeats in Microseconds

In a world of racing time,
Life unfolds in subtle chime.
Each moment feels like a race,
Yet we find our tranquil space.

Microseconds entwine our fate,
In the silence, we create.
Pulse of love, a rhythmic flow,
In this heartbeat, we both grow.

Every glance, a fleeting spark,
In the shadows, lights embark.
Time's dimension bends and sways,
Yet our hearts know the ways.

Caught in fleeting twilight hues,
Every touch ignites a muse.
Moments linger, soft and sweet,
As our hearts in rhythm beat.

So let the seconds gleam and shine,
In our dance, you're truly mine.
These heartbeats count the love we share,
In a world both bright and rare.

Invisible Entanglements

In the fabric of the unseen,
Lies a love that's evergreen.
Tangled threads of heart and mind,
In the void, our souls are twined.

Whispers float on cosmic breeze,
Connecting hearts with perfect ease.
In dark matter, soft and dense,
We discover our common sense.

Entangled thoughts, a silent sky,
With every laugh, we learn to fly.
In the quiet, truths collide,
Bound together, heart and pride.

We navigate through timeless space,
In invisible, warm embrace.
With every heartbeat, we ignite,
An unseen bond that feels so right.

So let us weave through shadows deep,
In this magic, dreams we keep.
Together, we find layers strong,
In each moment, we belong.

The Fabric of Intimacy

Threads of life, finely spun bright,
Woven close in the soft twilight.
In every layer, love resides,
An embrace where warmth abides.

Fabric stitched with laughter's grace,
Every moment a sacred space.
In the seams, our whispers blend,
An intimate tapestry to mend.

A patchwork quilt of heart's delight,
Holding stories through the night.
Softly sewn with hopes and dreams,
In this fabric, nothing's as it seems.

Each thread tells a tale unique,
In the silence, we softly speak.
Together, we'll weather life's storms,
In this closeness, our love forms.

Beneath the stars, let time stand still,
In this fabric, we find our will.
Stitched with care, our dreams unfold,
In the warmth of love untold.

Molecular Whispers

In the science of the heart,
Every atom plays a part.
Whispers carried through the air,
Electrons dance, a secret flare.

Molecules in tender space,
Forming bonds with gentle grace.
In each heartbeat, pulses flow,
Connecting us where love does grow.

Chemical reactions ignite,
In the stillness of the night.
With every glance, we intertwine,
In the rhythm, we align.

Gathered here in quiet bliss,
Every sigh, a fleeting kiss.
The universe has conspired,
To weave our fates, forever inspired.

So let the whispers gently swell,
In this dance, our hearts will tell.
With every bond, we drift and soar,
In this chemistry, we want more.

Threads of Connection

In whispers soft, we find our way,
A tapestry woven day by day.
Each moment shared, a gentle thread,
Binding our hearts where love is spread.

Through laughter and tears, we stitch it tight,
In shadows of doubt, we spark the light.
With every glance, a silent vow,
Together we stand, in the here and now.

The road ahead may twist and bend,
But hand in hand, we shall contend.
In vibrant hues, our stories blend,
A masterpiece that will never end.

And though the storms may rage outside,
Within our bond, we will not hide.
For even when the world feels cold,
In our embrace, warmth will unfold.

So here we weave, with love's intent,
A fabric rich, a life well-spent.
With every heartbeat, a new design,
Threads of connection, yours and mine.

Looking Deeper into Us

In the silence, where secrets lie,
I see reflections, you and I.
Eyes like windows, a soul exposed,
In every glance, our truth is posed.

Beyond the surface, we dive so deep,
In currents strong, our feelings steep.
Each layer peeled, reveals the core,
Unlocking dreams we can't ignore.

With every heartbeat, we intertwine,
A dance of spirits, so divine.
In quiet moments, we gain our sight,
Unveiling shadows, embracing light.

What lies beneath, the fears we hide,
In honesty, no need to bide.
We strip away the masks we wear,
In the depths, we find our care.

The journey shared, a sacred trust,
In vulnerability, we must adjust.
As life unfolds, we hold it dear,
Together we face what we might fear.

Micro-Forms of Tenderness

In fleeting moments, soft and small,
The little things can mean it all.
A gentle touch, a knowing smile,
In micro-forms, love spans the mile.

A shared glance in crowded space,
In quiet, we find our place.
The brush of hands, electric zing,
In tender gestures, feelings spring.

We gather memories like precious stones,
In the mosaic of soft tones.
With every sigh, with every laugh,
We map a path, our own little craft.

In the sigh of wind, in morning light,
The world awakens, feels so right.
Each moment cherished, glimmers bright,
A tapestry woven, day and night.

So here we stand, in simple grace,
Finding beauty in every trace.
In micro-forms, love does persist,
In tenderness, we always exist.

The Subtle Science of You

In quiet whispers of the night,
I study you, a pure delight.
The curves, the lines, a lovely art,
Each subtle move, it steals my heart.

With every glance, equations flow,
In the silence, our feelings grow.
The chemistry ignites a spark,
In shadows deep, we leave our mark.

The gravity of what we share,
Pulls me closer, lays us bare.
In pulses, rhythms, we align,
In every heartbeat, love's design.

So here we dance, in gentle sync,
In this space, we dare to think.
The subtle science of you and me,
A formula deep, a mystery.

And as we blend and intertwine,
I find that I am yours, you're mine.
In every laughter, every sigh,
In the chemistry, we will fly.

An Analysis of Affection

In the quiet whispers shared,
Layers unfold like petals rare,
A touch like softest feather,
It carries scents of warm air.

Each glance speaks a hidden verse,
Analyzing love's diverse,
The warmth that ignites our core,
A bond we cherish and immerse.

Through laughter, tears, moments frail,
We navigate our endless trail,
In every heartbeat, truth prevails,
Weaving tales where love won't fail.

Small gestures paint the grand design,
In every hug, our souls entwine,
Through storms and calm, we redefine,
What it means to intertwine.

So here's to every painted scene,
In this dance, we find the keen,
An analysis of affection,
In each heartbeat, love's direction.

Tiny Wonders of Togetherness

In the garden of small delights,
Every moment sparkles bright,
A shared smile beneath the sun,
Tiny wonders have begun.

From whispered dreams to soft caress,
Each memory, a sweet finesse,
Holding hands through gentle nights,
Finding joy in simple sights.

Side by side, in quiet bliss,
Every laugh, a precious kiss,
In the mundane, magic thrives,
Together, we ignite our lives.

A stroll beneath the starry sky,
With every step, our spirits fly,
In tiny wonders, we discover,
The beauty found in one another.

So here's to moments, soft and small,
In togetherness, we find it all,
A tapestry woven with care,
Tiny wonders, beyond compare.

Revelations in the Detail

In every shadow, stories hide,
Revelations in the detail abide,
A wrinkle in time, the depth of grace,
A world alive in a single space.

The rust of age tells tales untold,
In fractures and flaws, beauty unfolds,
A glance reveals the depths of sea,
In every grain, a mystery.

The corners of a smile convey,
What words might struggle to portray,
In each heartbeat, secrets dwell,
Revealing lives we know so well.

In broken paths, we find our way,
Out of shadows, into the day,
For every detail, a chance to see,
The essence of life's vast tapestry.

So here's to moments rich and deep,
In the details, we sow and reap,
Revelations shape our truth,
In the nuances lies the proof.

Enlightened by our Microcosm

In a world where we reside,
Microcosms, side by side,
In tiny realms, the wonders bloom,
Illuminated, dispelling gloom.

Through shared dreams and laughter's light,
We craft our universe, so bright,
In the small, we seek and find,
Connections, woven, intertwined.

Each moment shared, a spark ignites,
In our embrace, darkness takes flight,
With every heartbeat, worlds collide,
Enlightened by love as our guide.

In simplicity, our hearts expand,
Together, we create and stand,
A universe within our grasp,
In our microcosm, we clasp.

So cherish every fleeting hour,
In the little things, we find our power,
Enlightened by our sacred space,
In our microcosm, love's embrace.

Petal Pushing in the Laboratory

In glass jars, blooms reside,
Colors bright, side by side.
Gentle hands, they touch with care,
Science weaves through fragrant air.

Petals whisper, secrets kept,
In the lab, where dreams are swept.
Each one holds a tale to tell,
In the space where wonders dwell.

Beakers filled with vibrant hue,
Nature's work, both old and new.
Underneath the microscope's gaze,
Life unfolds in myriad ways.

Threads of pollen drift and dance,
In the light, they take their chance.
With each push, we seek to find,
The magic hidden, intertwined.

From petal soft to petal hard,
In this lab, they play their card.
With each stroke, we understand,
That beauty thrives at our command.

Passionate Particles

Tiny orbs in swirling space,
Chasing light with fervent grace.
Atoms spark with great delight,
In the dance of day and night.

Colliding thoughts, they intertwine,
Energy flows, sweet as wine.
In the heart of every soul,
Particles seek to be whole.

Radiant beams, they twist and curl,
Crafting dreams in a vibrant swirl.
Each collision, a new refrain,
In this cosmic, wild domain.

Through the void, their love transcends,
In the chaos, where all bends.
Passion fuels their endless flight,
As they journey through the night.

Energized by their intent,
Gathering strength, they circumvent.
In unity, they break apart,
Yet forever linked at heart.

Intimate Discoveries

In the quiet of the night,
Whispers float in soft moonlight.
Eyes that meet, a fleeting glance,
Every moment, a daring chance.

Curiosity ignites the spark,
In this air, we leave our mark.
Every touch, electric thrill,
In our hearts, the world stands still.

Layers peel, revealing truths,
In our laughter, find our roots.
With each breath, we draw so near,
In this space, there's nothing to fear.

Time slows down, we lose control,
Exploring realms that make us whole.
Mapping dreams upon our skin,
In these thoughts, we both begin.

Together, we uncover light,
In each shadow, pure delight.
Every secret softly shared,
In this journey, we are paired.

The Pulse of Sentiment

In the heartbeats of the day,
Rivers flow and thoughts betray.
Emotions rise, like tides at sea,
Telling tales of you and me.

Whispers caught in warm embrace,
Flavors sweet, we start to taste.
Every glance, a heartbeat's race,
In this dance, find our place.

With each sigh, the air will hum,
Actions speak where words are dumb.
In the stillness, hear the call,
The pulse of love connects us all.

Through the laughter, through the tears,
Memories weave through all our years.
Every moment, every breath,
In sentiment, there's no death.

Landscapes shift, but hearts remain,
In the rhythm, we find our gain.
The pulse that drives us, fierce and bright,
In this journey, our guiding light.

Particles and Passions

In the dance of atoms, we collide,
Electric sparks where hearts abide.
Particles in motion, a cosmic play,
Passions ignited, night turns to day.

Whispers of longing in the air,
Every glance a hidden dare.
Fragments of dreams entwined in time,
Our souls soar high, in rhythm and rhyme.

From stardust born, we rise and fall,
An instinctual pull, we're chained by the call.
Caught in the gravity of your embrace,
In this vast universe, we find our space.

With every heartbeat, the cosmos sways,
Ancient secrets in luminous rays.
Particles merge, in love they unite,
Together we shine, a dazzling light.

In the silence of night, we amplify,
The language of love, a soft lullaby.
Within us swirls a magical blend,
Particles and passions, a bond without end.

Analysis of Emotion

Beneath each smile, a story untold,
Layers of feelings, both timid and bold.
Fragments of joy, stitched with despair,
An emotional quilt, beyond compare.

Time, the canvas where passions bleed,
Moments captured, both sorrow and need.
Varying shades, the heart does paint,
Angels and demons, neither a saint.

A whisper of sadness, a laugh that glows,
In each twist of fate, the heart always knows.
Through the lens of love, we dissect the past,
An analysis of emotions amassed.

What stirs the heart, what makes it race?
Reflections of longing in time and space.
The tender pulse of a fragile chord,
In this study of feelings, we are restored.

With every breath, we delve so deep,
Into the depths where memories sleep.
The beauty of feeling, complex and raw,
An analysis of emotions, we draw.

Exploring Fragile Threads

In the fabric of life, we weave our dreams,
Fragile threads shimmering in moonbeams.
Every stitch tells a tale of its own,
A tapestry rich, but so easily torn.

Glimmers of hope in the silence we find,
Intertwined paths, two souls aligned.
We navigate storms with gentle care,
Holding on tightly, a promise we share.

Each thread a memory, delicate, rare,
As we uncover what's hidden with flair.
Exploring emotions that often collide,
In the intricate web where our hearts reside.

Unraveling moments both bitter and sweet,
With kindness, patience, our love is complete.
The fragility lingers but strengthens the bond,
A tapestry woven, our hearts correspond.

In this colorful dance, we embrace the light,
Facing the shadows, we ignite the night.
Exploring fragile threads, hand in hand,
Together we shape a love that will stand.

The Essence of Togetherness

In the quiet glow of dusk's embrace,
We find our peace in this sacred space.
Two souls entwined, like vines that blend,
The essence of togetherness, we transcend.

Through laughter and tears, we journey far,
Our hearts are guided by the same star.
In moments shared, our spirits ignite,
Creating a world that feels so right.

Hand in hand, we weather the storm,
Finding shelter in each other's arms.
With every heartbeat, we stand tall,
The essence of love, that conquers all.

In the whispers of night, our secrets unfold,
The stories of two, warm and bold.
Together we write, our chapter anew,
In the essence of togetherness, me and you.

With eyes that sparkle, we chase the dawn,
In the tapestry of life, we craft our song.
From the roots we nurture, our bonds expand,
The essence of togetherness, forever hand in hand.

A Study in Affection

With gentle words, we share our hearts,
In quiet moments, affection starts.
A whisper soft, a tender glance,
In love's embrace, we find our dance.

Two souls entwined, a sacred bond,
Through laughter's echo, we grow fond.
In every touch, warmth ignites,
Affection blooms in soft twilight.

A canvas painted with deep care,
In every memory, you are there.
Through storms and calm, we brave the way,
A study in love, day by day.

The sweet exchange, a knowing smile,
In your presence, I am worthwhile.
With every heartbeat, I discern,
The lessons of love, for which I yearn.

Bonded by moments, great and small,
In each other's arms, we find it all.
A radiant glow, our spirits blend,
In this study of love, there's no end.

Depths of Desire

In shadows deep, our passions sway,
A longing gaze that turns to play.
With every pulse, a crescendo grows,
In depths of desire, the heart knows.

A whispered breath, the air ignites,
In stolen glances, our souls take flight.
The heat of night, a fervent blaze,
In longing's grip, we drift in a haze.

Every touch, a spark, a flame,
In silent cries, we call each name.
Through tangled sheets, our secrets bare,
In depths of desire, we lay ourselves there.

Each heartbeat echoes, a thrilling call,
Bound by the night, we rise, we fall.
In every sigh, a promise made,
In the depths of our hearts, desires invade.

With every kiss, the world spins round,
In passion's grip, true love is found.
Through whispered wishes and dreams we chase,
In the depths of desire, we find our place.

Tendrils of Yearning

In twilight's glow, we seek the light,
Tendrils of yearning pull us tight.
A dance of souls in silent prayer,
In tender moments, we lay bare.

Through whispered hopes, we write our fate,
In every glance, we contemplate.
With hands entwined, we bridge the space,
Tendrils of yearning find their place.

A longing heart, a gentle plea,
In every dream, it's you and me.
With every word, a thread is spun,
Tendrils of yearning, two become one.

In moonlit nights, our shadows blend,
Through whispered truths, our hearts ascend.
In longing's dance, we find our song,
Tendrils of yearning, where we belong.

With hope as light, we'll forge the way,
In gentle gestures, we choose to stay.
Through every breath, we come alive,
In the tendrils of yearning, love will thrive.

Tiny Threads of Togetherness

In woven dreams, our lives connect,
Tiny threads of love reflect.
Through laughter's echo, joy aligns,
In tender moments, the heart defines.

With every smile, a bond is spun,
In simple gestures, two become one.
The rhythm of life, a soft caress,
Tiny threads of togetherness.

Through endless days and starry nights,
In shared glances, we feel the heights.
With every challenge, we find our way,
Tiny threads of love in bright array.

In warmth of hands, our spirits lift,
In every exchange, we find the gift.
The art of love, in silence dressed,
Tiny threads of togetherness, blessed.

In quiet strength, forever bound,
In each sweet memory, love is found.
With every twist, our stories blend,
In tiny threads, we will not end.

The Microcosm of Us

In the quiet corners of our hearts,
Where whispers of dreams softly start.
We weave together our hopes and fears,
A tapestry rich, through the years.

Moments fragile, like morning dew,
Captured in the light, just me and you.
In every glance, a story unfolds,
In the embrace of warmth, love beholds.

Time dances gracefully, ticking slow,
In microcosms, our feelings glow.
Each heartbeat a melody, sweet refrain,
Binding our souls like invisible chains.

In laughter shared, and tears that flow,
We find our strength, in ebb and flow.
Through storms and calm, we venture forth,
In the universe of us, a steadfast worth.

Each moment a star, bright in the night,
Guiding us gently, a beacon of light.
In the microcosm, forever entwined,
A symphony of hearts, beautifully aligned.

Glimmers of Serendipity

Beneath the canvas of swirling skies,
Serendipity whispers, softly it sighs.
A chance encounter, a fleeting glance,
Two souls collide in a cosmic dance.

Hidden treasures in the everyday,
Glimmers of magic in simple play.
Life's little surprises, sweet and rare,
Unfold like petals, in fragrant air.

In coffee shops or crowded streets,
Life's beautiful rhythm with heartbeats greets.
A sudden smile, a laugh that sways,
Turning the mundane into bright displays.

Follow those hints the universe leaves,
In strokes of fate, our heart believes.
Moments like these help us to see,
The beauty that blooms serendipitously.

So cherish the chance, the unexpected,
In life's rich tapestry, feel connected.
With each tiny spark, love's joy we sow,
In glimmers of serendipity, let us grow.

Heartfelt Science

In the chambers of the heart, equations reside,
Calculating love, with nothing to hide.
Each pulse a variable, each sigh a clue,
The science of feeling, profound and true.

Molecules dancing in a delicate waltz,
Connected by forces, no faults.
Physics of longing, chemistry's embrace,
In the lab of love, we find our place.

Through the lens of reason, we seek to explain,
But love is a mystery, defying the brain.
In formulas rigid, the heart breaks free,
Embracing the chaos, oh so beautifully.

Galaxies forming in the depths of the soul,
Navigating emotions, making us whole.
A symphony played on strings that bind,
In heartfelt science, true love we'll find.

So let us explore the wonders untold,
In the depths of our feelings, a journey bold.
With every heartbeat, a hypothesis new,
In the realm of the heart, we'll break through.

Feeling in Focus

When life blurs by, take a breath anew,
Find clarity in moments, just me and you.
In the stillness, we sharpen our gaze,
Discovering beauty in life's subtle ways.

The world around us hums and flows,
In focus, the heart of the matter glows.
With every blink, a snapshot we share,
In the lens of affection, we find repair.

Emotions captured, framed just right,
In shadows and light, our love ignites.
Through the fog, we seek the divine,
In feeling's embrace, our spirits align.

Silence reveals the whispers inside,
In feelings we trust, we no longer hide.
Each heartbeat a pulse of color and hue,
In the gallery of us, infinite view.

So let's cherish the moments so fine,
In the focus of feeling, let our hearts shine.
With open eyes, and a soul that feels,
In this sweet clarity, true love reveals.

Lenses of Longing

Through glass we seek to find,
The moments left behind.
Each glance a soft embrace,
A whisper in the space.

Desires wrapped in light,
Filling shadows of night.
Reflections stir our souls,
In fragments, we feel whole.

In every fallen tear,
Longings draw us near.
With visions crystal clear,
We chase what we hold dear.

These lenses show our hearts,
Where hope and dream departs.
Through focus, we can see,
Our truest memory.

With every single frame,
We play the silent game.
Longing's tender light,
Guides us through the night.

Clarity through Compression

In pixels, stories dwell,
Simple truths to tell.
Each filter sharp and bright,
Transforms the dark to light.

Beneath the layers worn,
New worlds shall be born.
Through colors blended tight,
We find the hidden sight.

A moment simplified,
Where shadows coincide.
With focus, find release,
In chaos, feel the peace.

Pixel by pixel formed,
In visions, we are warmed.
Compression gives us wings,
To soar with whispered things.

In this art, we breathe,
The truths we weave and leave.
Clarity bestowed,
In every path we rode.

Marvels of Micro-unions

Small wonders twist and weave,
In unity, they cleave.
Each grain tells a tale,
Where tiny dreams prevail.

In clusters, we unfold,
A story yet untold.
Connections bright as stars,
Across the unseen bars.

Microcosms flare,
Intricate designs declare.
Together, we unite,
In fragments of pure light.

The miracle of kin,
Endless love within.
In each minuscule bond,
A universe beyond.

Marvels in close range,
In every twist and change.
In stillness, we perceive,
Life's threads we interleave.

The Beauty of the Minuscule

In tiny folds of grace,
Life finds its rightful place.
A leaf upon the ground,
In silence, beauty's found.

The whispers of a breeze,
Dancing through the trees.
Each petal soft and bright,
A canvas kissed by light.

In shadows, small dreams glow,
Where few dare to go.
The details, bold and wise,
Open up our eyes.

Each crumb, a feast of thought,
In silence, lessons taught.
We tell our tales anew,
In tiny moments, true.

To cherish what is small,
Is to embrace it all.
In minuscule's embrace,
We find our rightful place.

Printed in the USA
CPSIA information can be obtained
at www.ICGtesting.com
CBHW070842031024
15215CB00094B/3217

9 789916 892992